A SORT OF LIGHT

Margaret Farrell

Published in 2012
by Poetry Workshop Publications
6 Selwyn Road, Cambridge CB3 9EB

ISBN 978 0 9566113 3 8

Illustrations by Tim Farrell
Cover image by Rhea Quien
Designed & produced by Arthouse Creative
www.arthousecreative.co.uk

ACKNOWLEDGEMENTS

For many years I was privileged to belong to the Cambridge U3A Poetry Writing group, convened by Robin Ivy, where we met fortnightly to read out our poems, and inspired each other with different themes and styles, always with much encouragement and generosity. I have also attended several poetry 'Masterclasses' at Madingley Hall near Cambridge, taught brilliantly yet firmly by Roger Garfitt. Most of the poetry in this volume has emerged from one or another of these settings.

I owe thanks to Robin and Roger and all the other companions in both groups. This booklet is dedicated to them all.

My thanks to my son Tim Farrell for the illustrations.

My thanks to Rhea Quien for the use of the cover design, taken from her film Dance of Light.

CONTENTS

IN THE HOUSE

THE MORNING HOUSE

The morning house
shines slants of sunlight on pale floors
and on the dusty panes, while
the quiet furniture
in rooms still dark
with curtains drawn
is ready to wake
and take its part in
matters of the day

So different from the house at night
where stillness is required
to shut life down
to bedded breathing darkness
enclosing secret dreams
which mock and jeer
at ordinary things of day.

And as I step on muted carpets
in the first cool spreading light of dawn
I greet the waking house and pull
aside the heavy curtains to let enter
thousands of dancing motes and rays
that spray life into every corner
as day begins to break.

GIFTS IN THE HOUSE

Like tigers
they crouch
beautiful but dangerous
on shelves, tables, window sills,
ready to spring at my heart,
tear it with golden claws –

objects of clay, of metal, convoluted shell, embroidered cloth,
exotic, brought from Bangalore, Kiev, Marrakech,
scooped from hot bazaars, souks, frenzied oceans, caves –

the touch of hands that gave them
invisible like air or glass
clinging to them
like fingerprints,
unique.

SCRAPS

Just scraps –
into the bin they go:
pieces of wool
and indigo;
three-inch threads,
combings of hair,
apple cores,
peelings of pear;
envelopes torn when contents read;
paper napkins, crumbs of bread;
filings of nails,
snippings of tin,
an old bus ticket and a rusty pin;
ends of ribbons that wrapped a parcel;
an old love-letter and a children's marble.

Suddenly, a shaft of sun
gleams on the scraps when the day is done,
and all that is dross and drear and old
instantly turns to precious gold
and the day that was ending in pieces and tatters
becomes a world of all that matters.

A SORT OF LIGHT

At four a.m. I wake and
prowl slippered through the sleeping house,
shuffling, and feeling, half-blind
along the empty corridor past the blank, hard windows

Until black no longer presses against my eyes,
as outside, shifting into life,
shapes become visible, grey and round —
appearing in a sort of light

And during that time,
between night and daylight
I could explore the mystery
that hints and beckons beyond the panes —

But, instead, I choose
to turn away, slip back to bed
and cover my eyes
so I can see familiar blackness once again.

IN THE GARDEN

ATTACHMENT

Seeking for things to love, I found
a yellow courgette flower,
so reckless in its open-ness,
so yawning with desire,

Yet already it is shrinking,
beginning to wither on its stalk –
and a faint scent of rotten-ness
teases the early autumn air:

Exuberance fades, reminding
that attachment must always end,
just as the over-blown rose
lets its petals slowly fall
on the cool silent loam beneath my feet.

BULBS

These bulbs cup fatly in my hand
waxy, white, inert:
I am instructed to plant them deep
in loamy soil
so the male trowel rudely pushes them
into the receiving earth
where worms and grubby insects
live their dark, blind lives.

And then the miracle begins,
slowly life takes shape
there, where we cannot see,
where grainy blackness
blocks out sight and sound.

How do they know (or is it feel?)
to make the green, the shy spikes
that push so softly
yet with such fierce certainty
into the cool spring air?

JANUARY

On a dark day the garden
beckons not at all –
the wet bricks
and the damp grass,
pools of last night's rain reflecting
the flat white sky
and a curtain of mist glooms all.

Yet a single blackbird
with a red berry in its beak,
and beyond the window
sprawled against the wet ivy
a spray of yellow jasmine
suggest that not all is melancholy
and spring may still defy the gloom.

MAY

Why can't it always be May?
when the green urgence pulls at the sap
that has filled
every blade and stem to bursting

And the whiteness
everywhere
looks like snow
but welcomes the sun
and blankets the fields
with lace laid dainty over the green

And the cuckoo calls and calls
its green notes
into the white air
while swallows swoop and dart
and larks spring up from nowhere

And the breathless air
and the green and the white
and the bees' humming
and the birds spinning
and our hearts yearning
dizzy us with joy.

AUTUMN ROSE

In amongst the now-bare hybrid teas,
whose rust-spotted leaves share the dark earth
with windfalls blackening on the ground,
bravely preens and primps
a frilly bloom
still deeply pink and orange,
shameless, pushing herself forward
on the thorny branch:

I remember my Aunt Nell,
married to a blind man –
her beauty was required
to be what it was:
it absolutely shouted –
even for us who could see,
we could not help but hear.

GHOST CARP

Deep in the clouded mud he used to lurk
under the weeds in the bottom of the pond,
until he chose to show himself
stealthily – his gold glinting back
rising to the shivering surface like a ghost
when everything was quiet,

    His power in his rareness,
    in his knowledge of our still watching
    our water god, shy and sublime,

Until one sharp morning we found a yellow fish
gasping in the border grass,
gills flickering, mouth scarcely kissing the air,
a puncture in his scaly side (made
by an unseen heron we surmised
who could not hoist his prey).

    Was this poor torn creature our water god?
    this fish, so still and wounded,
    lying on a plate of grass?

GAZEBO

In the July garden the green air hovers,
pushed by the weak sun
into dark corners
where plants are stifled,
stippled by lack of light

until the breeze quickens
and the tall plants begin to bend and quiver
in the sun now yellow as a knife,
now bullying boldly,
wilting the weed seedlings
which gasp for rain
promised by the clouds.

I watch from my safe gazebo, apart
and yet a part of all,
growing and decaying,

mourning the still moment.

BUTTERFLY

A butterfly with lace-edged wings
veined pale green like stitching in a muslin dress –
shares tall spikes of lavender with a bee,
busy in its striped pullover –
both going about their business
in the humming garden.

I do not think that
either of them can cause
things to happen
far across the world in jungled Cambodia,
or fabled Ankor Vat.

I think that the butterfly and the bee
exist here and now,
and their tiny moments
are all there is.

IN THE VILLAGE

STRANGER

Stranger in the village
lurks, hides behind bushes,
observes
the villagers
busy with dogs, wheelbarrows,
bicycles, deliveries,
riding horses, parking cars,
ringing doorbells, tapping panes.

How alien the stranger.

It is I.

COWS

The cows are in the fields now:
I see them through the windy cherry blossom,
lying heavy, brown, smooth,
so full of cream and munching slowness,
so fond of God and grass and buttercups.

They are not so foolish as
to ask questions.
They are just

there.

RIVER

Dark,
heavy as mercury
spilled from winter's thermometer,
slipping between muddy banks
from somewhere to nowhere,
reflecting bare branches
in its sullen mirror,
gelid, it scarcely moves,
yet carries
gleaming like snow

two perfect swans.

MAGPIE MARRIAGE

*'The spring gathering of magpies, the "great magpie marriage" of
the Rev. W. Damion Fox (1909) may well be concerned with pair
formation; Such gatherings are usually in early spring…both sexes
may display.'* (from Coombs, F., *The Crows*)

That's what they were doing, dashing into the river
like penguins plunging into ice,
dappling circles in the green
water, cleansing themselves,

flicking drops from pied breasts
as they climbed onto green
grass to flirt, to bow, to tilt their tails,
to sweep and swoop into the hanging willow tree.

Mafia magpies -- great on ceremony,
(never mind they are robbers, and worse)
don their best tuxedos,
pledge their vows to the priests of the air!

I want to be twenty-one again!
show it, flaunt it, black-and-white it –
knock their eyes out!
Frank Sinatra to sing at the wedding!

SWANS

Two swans white as sugar
stretch and bend
sweetly in unison
dipping their necks together
into the slowly swirling darkness of the pond
   while deep below unseen fish send circles upward

The pale swans dance together mutely
kissing and bending, twisting together,
rising and touching,
folding wings and bending necks
to nestle into the down of their bodies
   while deep below unseen fish send circles upward

The fish below are hunting, swimming,
snouting mud in the weedy bottom
touching, turning,
unseen, unknown
in the watery darkness
   while on the surface the swans are mating

BLACKBERRY PICKING

Black, multi-eyed creatures, almost alive,
hang gleaming, heavy with juice,
waiting to fall into the nest of my hand

as in the September sun hot upon my back
I grope my hand between the brambles,
pull my sleeve from the grip of the thorns,
as blood oozes thinly on my arm.
Decades of minutes
go by in solemn concentration.

Picking blackberries is what it's all about –
all is autumn-quiet in the cow-pasture,
except for muffled voices over the hedge,
indistinct and low,
rivals for black treasure.

Yet I do not pick each and every one –
I leave a few gripping the withering stalks –
the tiny, stunted ones, the red ones, still unripe,
nor those too low or too high –
and how I wish I had a walking stick
to pull those fat ones into my reach.

And as I stumble home past the afternoon cows,
berries rolling in my basket,
a memory lights up in a flash:

pushing a pram along these same hedgerows,
fifty years ago.

MEETING AT THE GATE

Why do I feel sad
when meeting friends by the meadow gate,
exchanging gossip and promises
to meet again,

and then, continuing on the path
through weedy grass
down to the sluggish river
on a gentle autumn afternoon

searching for the kingfisher
said to flit on its banks
flashing viridian wings
against the paling orange trees

and turning homeward now,
feeling a little chill in the air,
I catch a start of a tear in the throat
and a question: what next?

BEYOND AND AWAY

FLIGHT

Who gives us privilege to see
sun-capped and high-domed clouds
(not from beneath but far above)
and licks and spits of snow
on flattened hills
that from below would take a climb
far steeper than this seated ease?

Yet, that question 'who' reveals
our earth-bound groundedness and fear
of soaring height and airlessness,
and terror at the thought of metal wings
so heavy, yet so frail,
carrying us who cling to cushioned music,
darting films and meals on trays –
so utterly inert, not even beating
like the smallest sparrow on its path –
just gliding helplessly along
to something –
or to nothing –
we do not know.

CAIRO

I was in Cairo once, for a day –
pyramids behind me square-rooted in the sand,
Sphinx forgotten as a question –
and all I bought in Cairo
were gaudy paintings splashed on papyrus
for tourists wanting instant memories.

    From where I was I did not see the minarets
        nor the breasting domes against the blue Egyptian sky.

My aunt was in Newmarket once for a day –
buying skeins of wool for a jumper
red and blue, yellow and mauve
in the old marketplace
where bright wares lay beckoning on trestle tables

    And I believe she did not see
        the endless strings of shining horses
            wildly galloping past the white fences
                up the green hills.

HOLKHAM BEACH

Briefly, the day stands still –
    the sun sits in its high space,
    the sea, large and grey,
    frames the distance across flat sands –
voices stop, dogs cease their barking,
stillness seems forever.

Then the breeze starts up,
    sifting and pleating the grasses,
    figures begin to move
    tiny across the ruffled sands,
voices call and tremble on the salty air,
gulls dart and scream,
larks simmer in the sky
and we live again –

But something has been lost forever
    forever on the wind.

STREET SCENE

On a dirty street
dreary rain splashes
dwarfish wavelets of brown spume
and pavements grit-grey
sound to everyday
feet of weary citizens
winding and bobbing to-and-fro

past the Indian grocer's where
he tries to catch an extra penny
through wilting wares he sets outside
his failing shop with
tag-ends of old magazines,
shrivelled oranges, cycle patches,
soft onions and sweating cheese.

And then – in a battered bucket I see
wrapped in wrinkled cellophane,
like a beautiful child in a cheap dress –
ten white roses tinged with green,
breath-stopping in their innocence,
belying their prickly origins
in some money-maker's compost,

which catch my quotidian thoughts,
and make them trip and fall
through whatever ether they inhabit
to a ground of pure beauty
(ten white roses tinged with green)
where things are only of themselves, and
nothing more.

MORTALITY

Stumbling through tended olive groves
in distant Alpujarra
where I do not belong –
hoping, here, to make sense
of what is left of life
by encounters with another world,
yearning for ancient simplicity

I look down in the tumbled furrows,
see a tiny tangle of matted hair:
ferocity of nature suddenly exposed
by these indelible remains
of some poor animal who met its end.

I stoop to look more closely
and see – not stoat or pigeon –
but – head severed from body –
half eaten away, broken by the plough,
dusted by the pale, dry earth,
a mangled doll.

MEMORIES

APPASSIONATA

Humming in the background
the engine of my car
pumps its rhythm in F minor
while my hands tremble in tune
on the steering wheel

and disturbing the hum
like a pebble thrown into a stream
notes from a piano
escape through an open window,
tumble into the throbbing air
and fall into the tinnitus, drowning
the traffic buzz with

a memory of sounds, not words,
slicing through my neocortex
to an old part of the brain
where my father is still
sitting at his gleaming Steinway
playing the Appassionata.

MOTHER

Pale as night and
darker than the moon,
standing silent in the doorway
gazing at my hollow form,

she bewitched me
slipped into my helpless dreams
and departed soft as grass –
left a shadow thick in my blood,
pulsing lifelong through obedient veins.

MOTHER'S CLOTHES

Thin, insubstantial, they hang
on wire hangers like
limp bats silent in the daylight
or wrinkled moss, pale and dry.

They are not plumply filled by her,
nor likely to be, now,
as clothes are, an extra skin,
warm, soft, full of Person,

known still, but shrunken now.
There remains only a shed carapace,
feather-light, cast-off,
chrysalis, in fact,
of death.

REMEMBERING

When I want to ask how things were then,
in the old days,
the old days –
I turn to you in my mind
where your face shivers up like a misty breath
until I remember there's nothing left
but your body so frail,
lying in bed with a padded rail
waiting mute till they wheel you from bed to a chair,
wrapped in garments you never would wear
in the old days,

so I turn my thoughts to your sister
and hope that she might still recall
the places and people that both of you knew,
and where you went, and played, and who…
in the old days,
the old days:

the days of cousins and uncles and aunts,
days of horses and carts and leafy haunts,
of picnic cakes, the leaky boat,
the story of the house afloat,
the cousin who fell from the window ledge,
the car that crashed in the blackberry hedge…
and then I remember that she too lies
in a hospital bed with wrinkled eyes,
with her memory gone like a bird that's flown –

so that all that's left
of the old days,
the old days
are the scraps still swimming around in my head
until I too am laid in my bed.

JUMP ROPE

They used to play
one-two-three-o'leary
I didn't understand how
to run through the high arc of the rope
swung by two plump girls
one at each end smiling
lips smeared with forbidden licks of Tangee
one with a charm bracelet jingling on her wrist
the other with black patent-leather shoes
my mother said were vulgar

So I lurked in a corner of the dusty playground
pushing a round pebble into a hole
with my brown sensible shoe
while the boys played 'kick the can'
which I was not asked to join –

then I went to a new school
where I learned that 'jump' was 'sauter'
and 'kick' was 'donner un coup de pied'
and after that I travelled to Paris
where I strolled down the Boulevard St Germain,
drank black coffee at the Deux Magots

and had one hell of a good time!

THOUGHTS

FOREST

The dead trees do not fall
   at once.
Some lean on their green neighbours,
bending and twisting them,
tangling grey fingers round them
so that one cannot tell
the dead from the living.

Others stretch their proud skeletons
into the tall sky,
gleam straight as knives amongst the living trees,
not ready yet to fall or
crack or groan.

It may be a long, slow time
before any of them
lie gently down to make
   soft
the forest floor on which we tread.

ALWAYS

There used to be a sort of
Always
there, with the waves lapping
and the tide sucking
and the moon rising
and the sun setting.

At that time the deaths seemed small like dust
settled, almost invisible, on top of the eternal Things
until
suddenly too many lives vanished
and everything turned upside-down, and

now we are in a different place
forever,
where the waves are grey
and the tides are green
and the sun is blue
and the moon is black
and the rain is tears that fall
    Always.

DEAFNESS

Deafness enshrouds him like a blanket
perhaps of isinglass, or air,
invisible, untouchable,
but real as silk or wool,

or stiff cotton used to make
a strait-jacket of fabric
woven of unheard noises,
music, thunder, drums,

wind moaning in the trees,
trains howling in the distance
dogs barking, cows in the farmyard,
children shrilling in the playground,

knockings, shouting, whisperings –
all the same as nothing to him
as he sits and strains
to look, to hear
words through his eyes.

HEART SURGERY

He cupped your heart in his hands
removed it gently, put it in a steel dish
so that he could mend its broken valve
while the rest of your body
lay anaesthetised on the table
waiting patiently to receive its heart again.

There was no pain, not even in the
starched, white bed, where you were wheeled,
stitched up, receiving oxygen and nourishment
from snaking tubes and masks,
while the surgeon made his rounds
and pronounced you fit and well.

And the doctors and the nurses padded to and fro
while you lay there, all mended now,
heart beating, better than before,
your breast-bone healing every day--
and the surgeon made his rounds
and pronounced the operation a success

and I, who held your heart in my mind,
saw your familiar face again, unshaven, pale and grey,
(speaking breathless through the mask,
not conscious yet of your heart's strange journey,
unaware of its return to its accustomed place) –

Did I pronounce the operation a success?

SKELETON

Beached, white, tangled bone,
stark and gleaming in the fading light,
   skeleton of a whale

Once remote and dangerous,
churning the sea – its dark wavy home,
swallowing plankton, krill,
   lashing fragile ships that sailed too near.

The carcass recalls huge death
and fear that comes
   as darkness folds the edges of the day

And all bright, live, happy things
curl into sleep, or disappear
   into the terrible seas of night.

WOLVES

'There are wolves in the cupboard,'
the young child said,
sleep pressing against his eyes
(but not soothing his fears).
'No wolves,' said Mother, 'Just clothes.'

'There's a moth by the window!,'
the young child cried,
fear fixing his eyes to the spot.
'Not a moth, dear,' said Mother,
'just specks of light dancing on the curtains.'

'There's dark shadows in the corner,'
the young child whispered,
staring into the half-dark room,
'Only shadows, dear, nothing to fear –
they show us there is light somewhere.'

The child drifts off to peaceful lands, and
Mother slips to her cold-sheeted bed.
And then her fears begin:
the wolves, the moths,
the dancing lights, gibbering squeaks of sound,
and thickest thoughts that will not stop,
of loneliness and age and loss of hope
and death.

WHAT IS TRUTH?

From this window-seat I view the woods
and a slow, silver carpet of sedge
undulating to a softened edge,
and a bush with leaves of hammered gold
dancing in the fingers of the autumn wind –

yet, when I lean out,
hungry for treasure like Midas –
I see only a blank brick wall
cobbled with cold grey flints
seamed with broken mortar.

Stricken, I retreat into the darkened room
and find my mind grows slowly clearer
as I contemplate the sullen mirror

    that has given me the lie.

CHESTNUT TREE

By the meadow gate, under the chestnut tree
the wrinkled ground lies flat and brown,
sprinkled with blossoms
fallen from the high white candles –
tinged with pink like
little girls' party dresses.

Autumn is still a long way off,
when the ground will be thick with rustling leaves,
conkers glowing like treasure
beckoning to the party boys
who will mine them from their starry cases,
trampling the spent leaves underfoot –

I wonder – will you still be here?

CODA

WIDOWS

The world is crawling with widows
poisonous in their black garments
    trailing sorrow like yesterday's scarves
    clutching memories like old handbags

Where are they off to?
are they demented fools
    thinking they are joining dead husbands
    who left them long ago? –

Or perhaps they hope to join them
in some mad other world
    where ghosts wrap themselves
    around each other, in the dark.

IT'S YOU

The clunk of the front door:

'Is that you? He used to call –

'Yes, it's me!'

Our joke – who else would it be?

But, now, I am no longer 'You'

And I am no longer 'me' to him:

So, who am I, then?

I am no longer 'You',

I am only 'me' to 'me.'

LOSS

Why do they think it's any different –
loss?
now that we are growing old –
than for an inconsolable child
whose tears spill on his birthday,
whose aunts and uncles rush to heal,
to give him hugs,
books and toys –

Are we so different from distracted children?
we have no teddy bears
stuffed with consolation in their straw-filled fur,
only empty beds and daily tasks
which used to grace our adulthood
with busy meaning –
which now only serve
as dark games played in the glooming wood
before the fall of night.

YOU CAN GO NOW

You can go now –
Is that what I said to you?
    your arms so thin under the blankets,
    your breath fast as an engine,

I hope you felt my gentle hand
    stroking your bony shoulder,
    measuring slow time to a Buddhist refrain:
    '*May you be happy, may you find peace.*'

My heart was with you
in the shadowy room
    counting your breaths,
    counting my words:

'*You can go now*':
    did you hear me?
    Is that what I wished to say?
    when my heart wished you to stay –

You went, with a breath:
    I let you go:
    May you be happy, may you find peace.

ENDS

All things must have an end –
I'm not talking big things
divorce, miscarriage, death –

I'm thinking dinner at the Chinese restaurant,
races at the children's sports day,
meeting friends in the street,
conversations sliced by the telephone,
breakfast in the shadowed morning sun –

little deaths, each adding
to the final sum.